ST. PETER
CW00525935

Extreme Weather

Torrey Maloof

Published by Pearson Education Limited, 80 Strand, London, WC2R 0RL.

www.pearsonschools.co.uk

This edition is published by arrangement with Teacher Created Materials, Inc. for sale solely in the UK, Australia and New Zealand.

© 2015 Teacher Created Materials, Inc.

Text by Torrey Maloof

22 21 20 19 18
10 9 8 7 6 5 4 3 2 1

British Library Cataloguing in Publication Data
A catalogue record for this book is available from the British Library

ISBN 978 0 435 19470 3

Copyright notice
All rights reserved. No part of this publication may be reproduced in any form or by any means (including photocopying or storing it in any medium by electronic means and whether or not transiently or incidentally to some other use of this publication) without the written permission of the copyright owner, except in accordance with the provisions of the Copyright, Designs and Patents Act 1988 or under the terms of a licence issued by the Copyright Licensing Agency, Barnards Inn, 86 Fetter Lane, London EC4A 1EN (www.cla.co.uk). Applications for the copyright owner's written permission should be addressed to the publisher.

Printed in China by Golden Cup

Acknowledgements
We would like to thank the following schools for their invaluable help in the development and trialling of the Bug Club resources: Bishop Road Primary School, Bristol; Blackhorse Primary School, Bristol; Hollingwood Primary School, West Yorkshire; Kingswood Parks Primary, Hull; Langdale CE Primary School, Ambleside; Pickering Infant School, Pickering; The Royal School, Wolverhampton; St Thomas More's Catholic Primary School, Hampshire; West Park Primary School, Wolverhampton.

The author and publisher would like to thank the following individuals and organisations for permission to reproduce photographs and illustrations:
Photographs
(Key: b-bottom; c-centre; l-left; r-right; t-top; bck-background)
Cover Front:Alamy Stock **Photo:**Tom Wang, Back **Shutterstock** :Suppakij1017 b.
Alamy Stock Photo: Ilene MacDonald 7t, William Radcliffe/RGB Ventures/SuperStock 16-17bck, Nigel Cattlin 19, Ted Foxx 20-21bck, Andrew McConnell 21, Derek Croucher 22-23bck, US Marines Photo 26-27bck, Jochen Tack 27, **Getty Images:** KingWu/E+ 4-5bck, Dmbaker/iStock/Getty Images Plus 5, Harvepino/iStock/Getty Images Plus 6-7bck, _Huma/ iStock/Getty Images Plus 7b, 4x6/E+ 7c, BanksPhotos/E+ 8, Crisserbug/E+ 10-11bck, **Library of congress:** Library of Congress Prints and Photographs Division Washington, D.C. 20540 USA [LC-USZ62-043668] 24-25bck, **Newscom:** Brandon Wade/Fort Worth Star-Telegram/MCT 9b, Brian Branch Price/Polaris 31, **ScienceSource:** Roger Hill 2-3bck, Frant Lanting/Mint Images 6, Gary Hincks 9t, Julie Dermansky 11(d), Meckes/Ottawa 16, A.N.T. Library 23, **Shutterstock:** Lutsina Tatiana 11, ChameleonsEye 11(a)(b), Dustie 11(c)(f), Alexey Stiop 11(e), James Pearce 13, Harvepino 14-15bck, jean-Francois Manuel 15t, AMFPhotography 14, Paul Brennan 15b, Andrzej Kubik 18-19bck, Sven Hansche 22, HitToon 28,**NOAA:** 10b.
All illustrations: Teacher Created Materials(TCM).

Note from the publisher
Pearson has robust editorial processes, including answer and fact checks, to ensure the accuracy of the content in this publication, and every effort is made to ensure this publication is free of errors. We are, however, only human, and occasionally errors do occur. Pearson is not liable for any misunderstandings that arise as a result of errors in this publication, but it is our priority to ensure that the content is accurate. If you spot an error, please do contact us at resourcescorrections@pearson.com so we can make sure it is corrected.

Contents

Wild Weather

Imagine you have just finished setting up for a party in the park with your friends. It's a warm, sunny day. You have a huge water balloon fight planned. There is a rock-climbing wall to race up and delicious treats to share. You can't wait for the fun to begin!

Suddenly, the sky grows dark. The wind picks up, and your hair begins to blow in every direction. There's a bright flash of lightning in the sky. It's followed closely by a loud crash of thunder. Raindrops start falling from the sky. Minutes later, everything is drenched. The weather forecast did not mention a storm. But here it is. Is the party over? Maybe not – but it is definitely about to get wet!

Lightning strikes somewhere on Earth every second!

Meteorologists are people who study the weather. You may see them on TV presenting the weather forecast. They use tools such as radar and satellites to help them **predict** the weather. But sometimes it is hard to know what the weather will be.

There are lots of different types of weather. It can be hot or cold, windy or rainy. But in some places, the weather can be extreme! A tornado or a hurricane may blow through a city. A dust storm may rush through a town. Blizzards may cover entire cities in snow. This wild weather is dangerous. Meteorologists study extreme weather so that people who might be affected can be prepared.

a dust storm in Southern Madagascar

What's the weather?

March		🌡️	🌧️	☁️	🎏
1. mild with light rain	12°C	💧		◑	
2. rained most of the day	11°C	💧💧		●	←
3. partly sunny	9°C			◕	←
4. cool and windy	8°C			○	←
5. clear with a rainbow	10°C	💧		◑	→
6. mild, drizzle	10°C	💧		●	→

7

a car overturned by the power of a tornado

Terrifying Tornadoes

Have you ever heard of *The Wizard of Oz*? In this book and film, a tornado hits Dorothy's home. She gets swept up into the air and taken away to an enchanted land. This makes for an interesting story, but in real life, tornadoes don't carry people away to magical places! In fact, people need to seek shelter from tornadoes, because they are very dangerous.

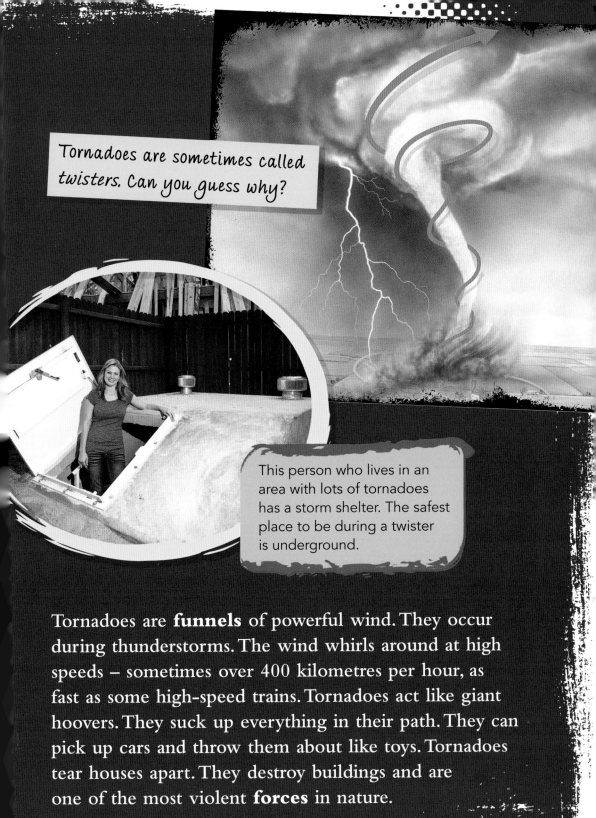

Tornadoes are sometimes called twisters. Can you guess why?

This person who lives in an area with lots of tornadoes has a storm shelter. The safest place to be during a twister is underground.

Tornadoes are **funnels** of powerful wind. They occur during thunderstorms. The wind whirls around at high speeds – sometimes over 400 kilometres per hour, as fast as some high-speed trains. Tornadoes act like giant hoovers. They suck up everything in their path. They can pick up cars and throw them about like toys. Tornadoes tear houses apart. They destroy buildings and are one of the most violent **forces** in nature.

Tetsuya Fujita was a tornado expert. The Fujita scale is named after him. Scientists around the world use this scale to rate tornadoes. It is based on the damage a tornado can cause. It also measures wind speed. The low end of the scale is EF0. This is a small tornado. The worst tornado is an EF5.

On 22nd May 2011, an EF5 tornado hit the town of Joplin, in Missouri in the USA. It was a Sunday afternoon. The weather was humid and hot. No one in Joplin knew that a powerful tornado was about to tear through their town. The massive twister flattened homes, ripped up streets and sent the wreckage flying. At one point, the tornado was over 1.5 kilometres wide! Over 100 people lost their lives. Many more were injured. The cost of the damage was enormous.

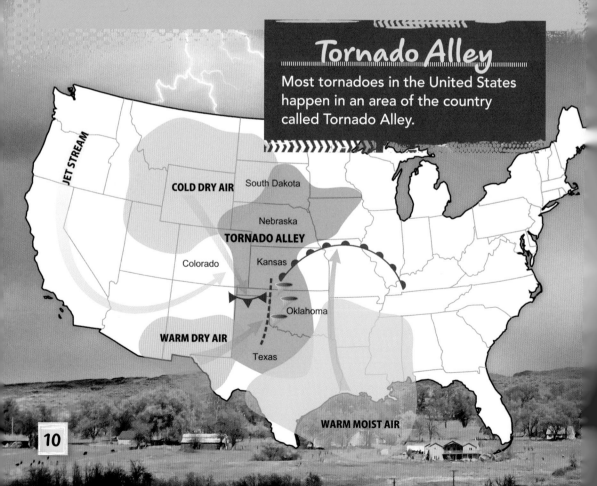

Tornado Alley

Most tornadoes in the United States happen in an area of the country called Tornado Alley.

JET STREAM

COLD DRY AIR

South Dakota

Nebraska

TORNADO ALLEY

Colorado

Kansas

Oklahoma

WARM DRY AIR

Texas

WARM MOIST AIR

The Fujita scale

Scale	Wind speed (kilometres per hour)	Wind speed (miles per hour)	Example
EF0	105–137	65–85	
EF1	138–178	86–110	
EF2	179–218	111–135	
EF3	219–266	136–165	
EF4	267–322	166–200	
EF5	greater than 322	greater than 200	

Savage Storms

The most violent storms on Earth are **tropical cyclones**. In some parts of the world they are called hurricanes, and in other parts of the world they are known as typhoons or cyclones. Whatever they are called, they can be very destructive.

Hurricanes form as tropical storms far out to sea. If they stay there, they're not so bad. Once they hit land they bring heavy rain and strong winds and cause a lot damage.

When a tropical storm reaches 119 kilometres per hour, it changes. It begins to pick up water vapour and forms clouds, which make a spiral shape. Inside the spiral, at the centre of the hurricane, there is an "eye". In the eye, the weather is calm. Outside the eye, the weather is wild and stormy.

2017
Hurricane Ophelia

In 2017 Hurricane Ophelia raged across the Atlantic Ocean to the UK.

Staying dry

If you live in an area that has hurricanes, you can stay dry – and safe – by following these steps:
- Listen to the radio or watch TV for warnings.
- Stay inside, close windows and doors, bring in pets and anything left outside.

The Atlantic hurricane season goes from 1st June to 30th November. In 2017, it was one of the most active seasons since records began in 1852. The three largest hurricanes came within weeks of each other.

In August, Hurricane Harvey caused massive flood damage in Texas and took many lives. In September, Hurricane Irma caused major damage and loss of life in the Caribbean and Florida, USA. Later in September, Hurricane Maria hit Puerto Rico and the country was without electricity for months. Many lives were lost.

2017
Hurricane Harvey

The naming system

The World Meteorological Organization gives hurricanes their names.

2017
Hurricane Maria

2017
Hurricane Irma

Disastrous Dust Storms

Have you ever wiped dust off a shelf or a television screen? Dust gathers quickly. It floats in the air before it settles on the ground or on an object. If you do not wipe it away, it will soon cover everything in your home!

Dust is made of many different things, including dry bits of soil, threads from clothing, pollen from plants and flakes of dead skin. Dust seems harmless enough until large amounts build up.

dust magnified under a powerful microscope

Ah-choo!

Sometimes, dust gets in your nose. If this happens, grab a tissue quickly! You are about to sneeze. Sneezing is your body's way of getting rid of dust.

Dust in your house isn't very dangerous. It may make your eyes red, or it may cause you to sneeze once in a while. Dust outside your house is another story.

Dust devils are like mini tornadoes that pick up lots of dust.

When there are strong winds in dry places, dust storms appear. Fierce winds kick up large amounts of dust. The dust travels up into the sky and is pushed by the wind. This creates large dust clouds. These clouds can cover entire cities and rise more than 10 kilometres into the air! They make it nearly impossible to see. The dust may contain harmful **particles**. This makes it very hard to breathe. It can also make people ill.

Dangerous droughts

A drought is a long period of dry weather. This means there is very little or no rain. Droughts are one cause of dust storms.

The corn plants on this farm are dying because of drought.

Dust storms often happen in deserts. Deserts are dry and have very few plants to help keep the sand in place. In places like this, winds can easily pick up sand and dust and create dust storms. This happened in Arizona, USA, in July 2012.

A dust storm that was 160 kilometres wide swept across the Arizona desert. The sun was completely blocked out. Aeroplanes could not land. Drivers could not see the road in front of them. The dust storm was so strong that it caused the power to go out. People's homes and businesses filled with dust. Swimming pools were turned into mud baths. The storm lasted for over 20 minutes. Luckily, no one was hurt, but everyone had a big mess to clean up!

a dust storm in Yuma, Arizona

Staying out of the storm

Dust storms can occur quickly. It is best to stay inside. But if you are caught outside in a storm, follow these tips:

- Wear a cloth over your nose and mouth.
- Wear glasses to protect your eyes.
- Apply petroleum jelly to the inside of your nose to keep it from drying out.
- Move to higher ground.
- Try to find shelter!

a dust storm in Eritrea

Brrr . . . Blizzards!

Snowball fights are fun. So is building a snowman. But too much snow can be a bad thing. Blizzards bring a lot of snow. And they bring it fast! A blizzard is a fierce winter storm with strong winds and very cold temperatures.

Blizzards happen when powerful winds called **jet streams** hit warmer air. The jet stream is pushed down while the warm air is pushed up. This creates snow and ice. Strong winds blow the snow. Those caught in a blizzard find it difficult to see. The fierce winds make the air feel even colder than it really is. This is called the wind–chill factor. If it is –1° Celsius outside, it can feel like it is -20° Celsius in cold, strong winds.

The Beast from the East was the name of a winter blizzard that raged across Europe from Siberia in 2018. London looked very different after it hit.

Frostbite

Frostbite happens when not enough blood flows to the hands, feet or ears. Skin tissue is destroyed. Sometimes, toes and fingers need to be cut off to cure the frostbite. Wearing layers can help prevent frostbite.

A blackout occurs when power is lost and all the lights go off. A whiteout happens during a blizzard when all you can see is snow.

One of the worst blizzards in history happened over 100 years ago, on the East Coast of the USA. Back then, predicting the weather was harder than it is today. No one knew when a storm was coming. It had been an unusually warm March day, but then, warm air from the Gulf of Mexico mixed with cold arctic air from Canada. A blizzard began.

After only a few hours there was about 140 centimetres of snow on the ground. Wind gusts blew over 137 kilometres per hour. The Great Blizzard of 1888 took the lives of many people. Today, meteorologists can warn people about approaching blizzards.

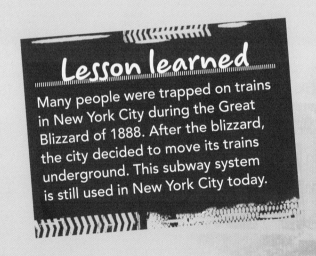

Lesson learned

Many people were trapped on trains in New York City during the Great Blizzard of 1888. After the blizzard, the city decided to move its trains underground. This subway system is still used in New York City today.

Be Prepared!

Weather can take many forms. On a sunny day, the sky can be filled with fluffy clouds. But the water in the air can quickly turn into rain, hail or a flurry of snowflakes. A cool breeze can feel refreshing on a hot day. But wind can become wild and dangerous in a hurricane or a tornado.

People boarding a plane to escape a hurricane in the Philippines.

The weather is constantly changing, but if you are prepared, you can handle any weather Mother Nature may throw your way!

Let's Try It!

How does a tornado move? Experiment and find out!

What you need

- 2 large plastic bottles
- duct tape
- food colouring
- glitter (optional)
- scissors
- water

What to do

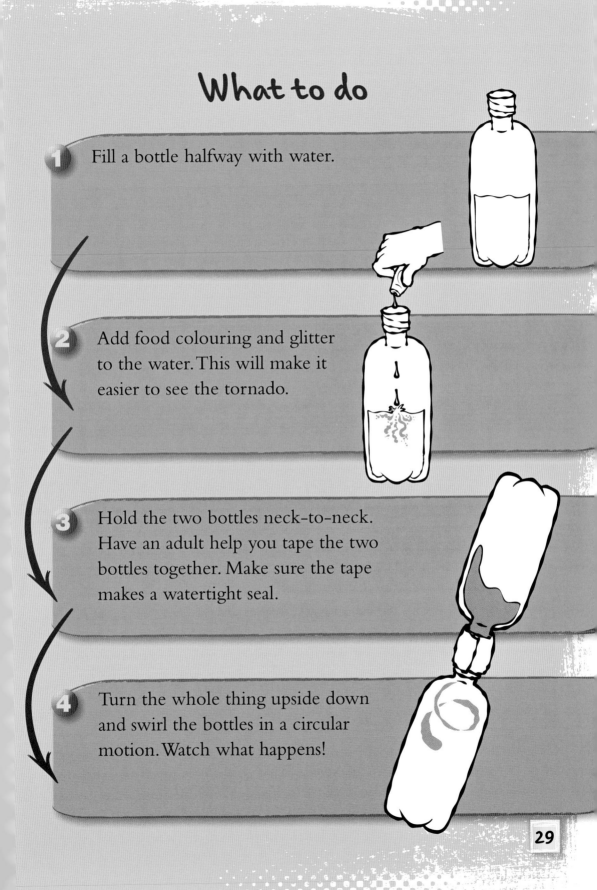

1. Fill a bottle halfway with water.

2. Add food colouring and glitter to the water. This will make it easier to see the tornado.

3. Hold the two bottles neck-to-neck. Have an adult help you tape the two bottles together. Make sure the tape makes a watertight seal.

4. Turn the whole thing upside down and swirl the bottles in a circular motion. Watch what happens!

Glossary

forces – strengths or powers

funnels – things shaped like hollow cones

jet streams – strong currents of fast winds high above Earth's surface

meteorologists – people who study the atmosphere, weather and weather forecasting

particles – very small pieces of something

predict – to say that something will or might happen in the future

tropical cyclone – a circular storm that forms over warm oceans

vapour – a substance in the form of a gas

Index

Your Turn!

Wacky weather

Have you seen a lightning storm? Maybe you've been caught in a blizzard. What extreme weather have you experienced? Write a journal entry about a time you saw some wacky weather. Draw a picture to go with your journal entry.